MARILYN MONROE

" QUOTE UNQUOTE "

MARILYN MONROE

"Quote Unquote"

Janice Anderson

CRESCENT BOOKS
NEW YORK • AVENEL

ACKNOWLEDGEMENTS

The author and publisher acknowledge the following references, where
many of the quotes in this book can be found.

Janice Anderson, *Marilyn Monroe,* Optimum Books, London, 1983. **Peter Brown** and **Patte Barham**,
Marilyn: The Last Take, William Heinemann, London, 1992. **Michael Conway** and **Mark Ricci** (eds.), *The
Films of Marilyn Monroe,* Citadel, New York, 1964. **Neil Grant** (compiler), *Marilyn In Her Own Words,* Pyramid
Books, London, 1991. **Fred Lawrence Guiles**, *Norma Jeane: The Life and Death of Marilyn Monroe,* Granada,
London, 1985. **Norman Mailer**, *Marilyn,* Hodder and Stoughton, London, 1973. **Pete Martin**, *Marilyn
Monroe,* Frederick Muller, London, 1956. **Norman Rosten**, *Marilyn, A Very Personal Story,* Millington, London,
1974. **Bert Stern**, *The Last Sitting,* Orbis Publishing, London, 1982. **Anthony Summers**, *Goddess: The Secret
Lives of Marilyn Monroe,* Gollancz, London, 1985. **William J. Weatherby**, *Conversations with Marilyn,* Robson
Books, London, 1976.

PICTURE CREDITS

Camera Press, London pages 74 (Lawrence Schiller), 79; **Ronald Grant
Archive** back cover, pages 10, 12, 14, 16, 21, 28, 30, 32, 36, 39, 40, 46, 47, 49,
53, 54, 62, 67; **Hulton Deutsch Collection** pages 11, 13, 56; **Pictorial Press**
front cover (Gene Gorman), pages 15, 20, 29, 34, 48, 55, 60, 70; **Popperfoto** page
69; **Range/Bettman/UPI** pages 44, 72and 80; **Rex Features** pages 2 (Sipa), 8,
23, 24, 51 (Sipa, Tom Ewell), 58, 64, 77.

This 1995 edition published by
Crescent Books, distributed by Random House Value
Publishing, Inc.,
40 Englehard Avenue, Avenel, New Jersey 07001.

Random House
New York • Toronto • London • Sydney • Auckland

A CIP catalog record for this book is available from the
Library of Congress

Publishing Manager: Sally Harper
Editor: Barbara Horn
Design and DTP: Crump Design

ISBN 1 85813 831 0

Printed in Italy

CONTENTS

THE CAMERA'S DARLING

'I want to grow old without face-lifts ... I want to have the courage to be loyal to the face I have made. Sometimes I think it would be easier to avoid old age, to die young, but then you'd never complete your life, would you? You'd never wholly know yourself.'

FACING PAGE: *Marilyn Monroe in a publicity shot for* ALL ABOUT EVE *(1950), in which she first joined the stars in a small but essential role.*

Iᴛ's sᴘʀɪɴɢ in Beverly Hills, Los Angeles, just a few days before the 1994 Academy Awards ceremony. The great American magazine *The New Yorker* is throwing a party in the garden of the Bel Air Hotel to launch a special issue devoted entirely to the film industry. Everyone who is anyone in Hollywood is there: Steven Spielberg, Robin Williams, Whoopie Goldberg, Emma Thompson, Shirley MacLaine, Angelica Huston, presidents and chairmen of film production companies, writers of world stature like Gore Vidal … Looming over them all in the glamorous marquee is a huge collage of photographs of Marilyn Monroe. Larger than life, her wonderful curves encased in a skin-tight, halter-necked dress, her white-blonde hair a riot of curls about her head, Monroe dances with abandon, throwing herself joyfully into the business of posing for the camera.

Photographer Richard Avedon took the pictures nearly forty years ago. Marilyn Monroe has been dead for more than thirty years. Yet the results of their day's work in a New York studio in 1957, given their first public showing in *The New Yorker* in 1994, are not there to remind the world of Monroe's special magic, so much as to reinforce our knowledge of it.

Lᴇꜰᴛ: *Marilyn Monroe remains a very special movie star; on-screen, she continues to seem gloriously alive.*

Of all the beautiful women who have become 'screen goddesses' during the hundred-year history of the cinema, Marilyn Monroe is the only one whose vivid image remains instantly recognisable to millions of men and women, young and old, throughout the world. Each new generation of movie-goers and film commentators seems to discover her afresh, virtually re-inventing her image to suit the fashion of the time and there have been many imitators of the Monroe 'style', both during her lifetime and since.

Paradoxically, it is the failure of her imitators to come near to capturing Monroe's essential nature that does most to give us a clue to the reason for the extraordinary cult that has grown up around her. Most imitators manage to achieve a physical approximation of Monroe's obvious sex appeal. What none of them has been able to conjure up is the waif-like vulnerability and delicious innocence that, allied to her undoubted sexuality, made her unique.

An important factor in the creation of the Monroe legend was the rare ability she had to transform herself from the quite ordinary to the wholly extraordinary in front of the camera lens, particularly the lens of the still camera. Commenting on his photographs in *The New Yorker,* Richard Avedon affirmed what other photographers have said: Marilyn Monroe was much more at ease in front of the still camera than the movie camera. 'She spent hours in the dressing room, creating the invention that was Marilyn. The moment she came out to work she never looked in the mirror again … With the help of white wine she released herself, through her complete discipline, into the necessary wildness that would achieve Marilyn Monroe,' recalled Avedon in 1994.

Marilyn herself would not have argued with Avedon's contention that she deliberately created her own image. Photographer Eve Arnold remembers Marilyn saying, in effect, 'Let's make a Marilyn' at the start of their many photographic sessions together.

Eve Arnold found Marilyn Monroe a joy to work with. Even when a session started out badly – Monroe hours late, her face heavy with the effects of the night before, she could suddenly become effervescent, radiant, ready to create an image to please her public. She once defended her wearing of heavy make-up in public by saying that

---

'I am not interested in money. I just want to be wonderful.'

---

she put it on for the guy at the back of the crowd on the other side of Times Square. Her still-camera photographs were also made for all the guys at the back of the crowd, all over the world. It was as if she felt that still photographs allowed her to reach out more directly to her 'public' than did her work in movies.

It was largely through the lens of the still camera that Monroe's 'screen goddess' image was created. From her earliest teenage forays into the world of photographic modelling, she enjoyed working on pin-up and cheesecake pictures. Later, as she became a famous movie star, she spent

'Fame is fickle and I know it. It has its compensations, but it also has its drawbacks and I've experienced them both.'

hours with the studio's publicity photographers, taking immense pains over the quality of the glamour portraits the front office and PR men would be sending to magazines, newspapers and other film PR offices all over the world.

At the outset of her career her pin-up pictures involved just her and the photographer. Later on, of course, 'making a Marilyn' with the world's best-known movie star was a very different operation. Studio and photographer, who would probably be one of the best and most highly paid in America, would be booked months in advance, there would be flowers and champagne on ice awaiting the arrival of the star (likely to be hours late), her own make-up man, 'Whitey' Snyder, would be in attendance and Frank Sinatra records would be playing soothingly in the background.

Marilyn Monroe's last such photographic sessions, done in a hectic twenty-day burst less than two months before her death in August 1962, provided the world with the final burnishing of the image that has remained so potent ever since. It was an image very much controlled by Marilyn herself. She sifted through the thousands of prints and negatives, scoring through the bad ones with a hairpin or a red pencil, choosing the very few that would be published in such major magazines as *Vogue* and *Paris Match*. In fact, she was mounting a determined counter-attack against the studio bosses who had just sacked her from her last film, using a great publicity campaign to put her side of the argument, to get her accepted as the major movie star and actress she knew herself to be.

The pictures that resulted from this photographic campaign, most of them not published until after her death, became a

'With fame, you know, you can read about yourself, somebody else's ideas about you, but what's important is how you feel about yourself — for survival and living day to day with what comes up.'

major part of the Monroe legend. They show a beautiful, desirable and wonderfully vital Marilyn, more mature but also more warm and outgoing.

Among the best-known of this series of photographs was a group taken by *Vogue* photographer Bert Stern of a laughing Marilyn holding a thin gauze scarf in front of her naked body. Then there were Hollywood photographer Douglas Kirkland's pictures of her lying on a white bed, with white satin sheets apparently her only covering. In delightful contrast was a series of natural, unposed pictures taken by journalist George Barris on the beach in front of Peter Lawford's house, with Marilyn wrapped in a heavy Mexican sweater and holding a glass of champagne, her wind-blown hair haloed against the late-afternoon sun and the sea.

If, as Richard Avedon suggested and these photographs appear to confirm, Marilyn Monroe invented herself, she was extraordinarily successful, for the invention has proved impervious to changing taste, style and fashion. At the Bel Air Hotel party in 1994 her pictures seemed totally in tune with the atmosphere of the occasion and with the fascinating world that is Hollywood.

RIGHT: *Even in costumes that are not (by today's standards) particularly revealing, Marilyn radiated a carefree sexuality.*

'I knew I belonged to the public and to the world, not because I was talented or even beautiful, but because I had never belonged to anything or anyone else.'

NORMA JEANE TRANSFORMED

'Some of my foster families used to send me to the movies to get me out of the house, and I'd sit all day and way into the night … I loved anything that moved up there and I didn't miss anything that happened. I dreamed of myself walking proudly in beautiful clothes and being admired by everyone and overhearing words of praise.'

FACING PAGE: *Few who knew her in her deprived childhood would have recognized Norma Jeane Baker in this glamorous studio portrait of Marilyn Monroe, made in the late 1940s.*

MARILYN MONROE once remarked 'Los Angeles was my home ... so when they said "Go home!" I said, "I am home."' Marilyn Monroe always felt her roots to be there. She bought her only house in Los Angeles a few months before she died, and she retreated to it to gather her forces after her final row with Twentieth Century-Fox.

Marilyn was born on 1 June 1926. The name put on her birth certificate was Norma Jeane Baker. Her mother, Gladys

---

'I'm a waif. I'm not calling myself an orphan.'

Baker Mortensen, had reverted to the name of her first husband (and father of her two daughters) after her second husband, Edward Mortensen, had disappeared just months after their marriage in 1924. Neither Baker nor Mortensen was Norma Jeane's father. The most likely candidate was Gladys Baker's most recent lover, C. Stanley Gifford, a salesman for the film cutting laboratory where Gladys had been working before Norma Jeane's birth.

Gifford offered Gladys cash to help her sort out her position, but refused to have anything else to do with the baby, which may have contributed to her later mental breakdowns.

Norma Jeane spent her infancy and childhood in foster homes in Los Angeles. Until increasing mental breakdown took Gladys Baker into an asylum, she carried on her job as a film-cutter, earning money to pay for Norma Jeane to be looked after by foster parents. There was one long stay in an orphanage, which was to leave an indelible scar on Marilyn Monroe's emotional make-up, but on the whole her childhood appears to have been passed in the care of people who, though they may not have been able to give her the love she was to crave throughout her life, gave her reasonably comfortable homes and surroundings.

All this took place on the fringes of the most glamorous place in the world, Hollywood. While Norma Jeane never got to see the great stars, she picked up scraps of gossip about them from her earliest years, sometimes in the cutting laboratories where her mother worked. She was once taken to look at the prints of stars' hands and feet set in the pavement outside Grauman's Chinese Theater.

She spent many of her Saturday mornings going to the movies. She became an avid reader of fan magazines, studying the glossy studio portraits of the great stars intently. From the moment she began working in the movies she was very aware of the importance of publicity – and of the importance of handling it herself. As she once said in an interview, 'I might never see … an article and it might be okayed in the studio. This is wrong because when I was a little girl I read signed stories in fan magazines and I believed every word the stars said in them. Then I'd try to model my life after the lives of the stars I read about.'

The teenage Norma Jeane's ambitions were set on becoming one of the starlets or pin-ups she also read about in the fan magazines. She did not think that she had a beautiful enough face to become a real movie star. She soon learned, however, that she had the figure to make a successful pin-up girl. She was about fourteen when she began noticing the reactions of the boys at Van Nuys High School to her figure-hugging sweaters.

Soon, her current guardians, Grace and 'Doc' Goddard – old friends of Gladys Baker, and, with Grace's aunt, Ana Lower, the nearest Norma Jeane got to having

'No-one ever told me I was pretty when I was a little girl. All little girls should be told they are pretty, even if they aren't.'

'The truth was that with all my lipstick and mascara and precocious curves I was as unresponsive as a fossil … I used to lie awake at night wondering why the boys came after me.'

loving relations — were worried about their physically precocious charge. They decided that the best solution to the problem of what to do with Norma Jeane was marriage to James Edward Dougherty, the good-looking son of the family next door. Jim and Norma Jeane were sent out on dates and in June 1942 they were married. Norma Jeane was just sixteen years old.

While the first few months of the Dougherty marriage were carefree and happy enough, the Second World War soon caught up with them. Jim Dougherty enlisted and was eventually sent to sea, ending up as far away as Australia. Norma Jeane moved in with her in-laws, but found that this was not too much to her liking. She was feeling stirrings of independence and decided to do something for the war effort by getting herself a job. She went to work in an aircraft-parts factory in Los Angeles, at first packing parachutes to be attached to miniature target planes, then spraying fuselage parts, a job that involved wearing overalls, which young Mrs Dougherty filled delightfully well. She did her job well, too, winning a certificate for 'excellence on the job'. In fact, when an Army photographer called David Conover from the First Motion Picture Unit (commanding officer: Ronald

LEFT: *On the day of her wedding to Jim Dougherty in June, 1942.*

Reagan) came to the factory to take pictures of women doing war work for *Yank* magazine, Norma Jeane thought that it was winning the certificate that had got her singled out to be photographed. Conover, excited by what he saw on film, went back to Norma Jeane's factory and arranged more photographic sessions with her.

Though she did not realize it then, there would be no going back to the old life for Norma Jeane Dougherty. From this very first photographic opportunity, she was, in effect, on her way. Those first photographs were enough to show that, as far as any relationship with a camera was concerned, Norma Jeane was unique.

By June 1945, with husband Jim still in the navy somewhere off the coast of South America, Norma Jeane was on the books of the prestigious Blue Book Modelling Studio and Agency, whose head, Emmeline Snively, was to become the first of her many guides and mentors. Norma Jeane, suppressing the fact of her marriage because she felt it might endanger her chances in a modelling career, began attending modelling classes and taking on more and more assignments.

When Jim Dougherty returned from the war, he found there was no room for him and his wife divorced him in Reno in 1946.

LEFT: *Norma Jeane with her half-sister, Berneice Miracle.*

Shortly after that she began lightening her hair because golden blondes were what the Blue Book Agency's clients wanted. By now, she was very busy, not just working for clients like Douglas Aircraft and Holga Steel, but also doing pin-up and cheesecake pictures for the covers of magazines with names like *Laff, Titter* and *Pageant,* most of them girlie magazines for barbers' waiting benches and garage mechanics' washrooms.

Some of the best-known photographs from this period in Norma Jeane's life were the work of a young Hungarian war refugee called André de Dienes. He had asked Norma Jeane to marry him, but she was

'My marriage [to Jim Dougherty] brought me neither happiness nor pain. My husband and I hardly spoke to each other. This wasn't because we were angry. We had nothing to say.'

recently divorced, free and independent, and wanted things kept that way – for the time being. De Diene's lovely photographs of her, published on the covers of several big-circulation magazines, promoted her ambitions at the expense of his desires.

By now both Norma Jeane and Emmeline Snively had their eyes set on a movie test. Miss Snively, who had already been casting about for a more suitable name for her most successful client, was probably the author of the story that appeared in the gossip columns to the effect that Howard Hughes, recovering in hospital from a serious air crash, was moved to sit up and demand of his aides the name of the girl on the cover of *Laff* magazine. If 'Miss Jean Norman' was exciting enough to interest Howard Hughes, then surely other film executives should be interested, too.

Shortly after this, in July 1946, Norma Jeane walked through the famous gates of Twentieth Century-Fox Pictures. She had an appointment with Ben Lyon, casting director and head of new talent with the studio. Ben Lyon liked what he saw very much. She seemed a decent sort of girl. When he saw the results of the film test he had arranged, he made some mental readjustments. The decent sort looked very good on film. She had plenty of 'flesh impact' and, said cameraman Leon Shamroy, 'sex on a piece of film like Jean Harlow'. Darryl Zanuck, head of Twentieth Century-Fox, was also impressed by the screen test, and a week after she did it, Norma Jeane Dougherty was told that the studio had decided to give her a short contract, with an option to renew. Ben Lyon said that her name would not do. He suggested Marilyn, thinking of the musical comedy star, Marilyn Miller, to whom he had once been engaged. She came up with her mother's maiden name, Monroe, for her surname.

So, from August 1946, Hollywood had a new starlet on the lot: twenty-year-old Marilyn Monroe, still doing pin-up and glamour photography, as she always would, but now swapping her modelling classes for acting courses.

LEFT: *When Norma Jeane was before the camera, the pretty girl was transformed into a lovely creature, radiating vitality.*

ROAD TO STARDOM

'My illusions didn't have anything to do with being a fine actress. I knew how third rate I was. I could actually feel my lack of talent, as if it were cheap clothes I was wearing inside. But, my God, how I wanted to learn, to change, to improve! I didn't want anything else. Not men, not money, not love, but the ability to act.'

MARILYN MONROE was just one of at least three dozen beginners taken on by Twentieth Century-Fox in the late summer of 1946, and she did not work on a studio sound stage until well into 1947. The newly blonded Marilyn Monroe was just too inexperienced to be risked in anything more than walk-ons.

Marilyn spent her time diligently attending drama classes at the Actors' Lab, and voice, dancing and exercise classes on the

'I'm going to be a great movie star some day.'

studio's lot. She also spent hours with the studio's still photographers or with leading photographers like Bernard of Hollywood, posing for the pin-up and cheesecake pictures that were essential to the studio's publicity machine. Because she was pretty and bubbling over with good humour and pleasure in her work, the publicity department also used her for public appearances.

After about six months of this, Marilyn Monroe was at last told to report for work on a film. It was recently discovered that

Marilyn Monroe was credited with an appearance in a Betty Grable film, *The Shocking Miss Pilgrim,* released in 1947. Until then, a film called *Scudda Hoo! Scudda Hay!* was always considered to have been the first to have provided on-screen work for Marilyn Monroe. Most of Marilyn's part in it ended up on the cutting-room floor. All that was left was a very long shot of her in a rowing boat with another girl.

Since the release of *Scudda Hoo! Scudda Hay!* was delayed until 1948, the second film Marilyn worked on, *Dangerous Years,* appeared first. Once again, Marilyn's contribution to this drama of juvenile delinquency was slight and what she did impressed no one. Twentieth Century-Fox's head, Darryl Zanuck, had never had a high opinion of Marilyn's abilities, and when the option on her contract came up for renewal in August 1947, the studio decided they did not want to sign her. It is possible that her

'Only the public can make a star. It's the studios who try to make a system out of it.'

relationship at this time with seventy-year-old Joseph M. Schenck, co-founder of Fox with Zanuck and still the studio's executive producer, had something to do with Zanuck's decision.

Whatever the reason, Marilyn Monroe had several lean years ahead of her. It may have been Schenck who used his influence to get Marilyn the interview at Columbia Pictures that resulted in a six-month option contract, signed in March 1948. The feeble B movie Columbia put her into that year, *Ladies of the Chorus,* included a leading part for her and allowed something of the Monroe figure to be seen. She had one scene prominently placed in the chorus line, wearing a slinky black dress split to the thigh and singing a song called 'Every Baby Needs a Da Da Daddy'.

Apart from the film, there were two pluses for Marilyn in her contract with Columbia. The studio sent her to their acting coach, Natasha Lytess. A solid relationship grew up between the two women; Lytess was the first real ally Marilyn found in the tough world of Hollywood and a good friend, besides. Lytess soon discovered two important things about her latest student: the rather plump, apparently talentless girl was transformed in front of the camera, and she had a relentless desire to succeed. Lytess became the cornerstone in the creation of Marilyn Monroe, actress.

The other plus in Marilyn's work for Columbia was her meeting with the studio's musical director, Fred Karger, who spent hours coaching her in the songs she sang in *Ladies of the Chorus.* If the *Motion Picture Herald* was able to call Marilyn's singing 'pleasing', this was largely due to Karger's work on her voice, which was small, though it could hold a tune.

Marilyn appears to have fallen in love with Karger, while he was interested enough in her to take her to meet his family and to take her to concerts, the theatre, to dinners and dancing. He even found her a better apartment than the one-room studio where she lived with her dog and two hundred books. Eventually, their relationship ended, with Karger going on to marry actress Jane Wyman. By this time Marilyn's relationship with Columbia had also ended, for the studio, like Fox, did not see enough in her to want to take up their option on her contract.

She returned to the pin-up and cheesecake work. At one point in 1949 she was so short of money she could pay neither her rent nor the payments due on her car.

FACING PAGE: *With Adele Jergens in* LADIES OF THE CHORUS *(1948).*

RIGHT: *A portrait of Marilyn Monroe from her early modelling days.*

When an old friend, photographer Tom Kelley, offered her fifty dollars to pose in the nude, something she had previously refused to do, she agreed. Kelley's wife assisted, the session proved relaxed and untroubled, and Marilyn used the money to retrieve her car. That was the end of that, as far as she was concerned.

From her own account, Marilyn got her next film part herself. Hearing that a sexy blonde was needed at RKO for an independently produced Marx Brothers movie, she telephoned the producer and made an appointment. Hollywood legend has it that she only had to walk across producer Lester Cowan's office in front of Groucho Marx to get the job. The film, *Love Happy,* released

'I learned to walk as a baby and I haven't had a lesson since.'

by United Artists in 1950, was nothing special. It was the first the once-great Marx Brothers had made together for some years, and Groucho added a line or two of dialogue specially suited to Marilyn's talents:

RIGHT: *In LOVE HAPPY (1950), Marilyn acted alongside Groucho Marx, who added some dialogue with Marilyn in mind.*

'I had to wriggle across a room. I practised jiggling my backside for a week. Groucho loved it.'

'Men keep following me all the time', she complained to private detective Sam Grunion (Groucho) in her little-girl whispery voice, before walking out of his office in a way that left no doubt as to why she had the problem.

Lester Cowan sent Marilyn on a coast-to-coast publicity trip for *Love Happy,* which gave her her first glimpse of New York. It allowed New Yorkers their first glimpse of Marilyn, too: 'Hollywood's hottest new property cooling off in New York', said one newspaper headline over a photograph of her. Amidst all the newspaper interviews, publicity appearances and radio chats she did in New York, she found time to go to Jones Beach with her old friend André de Dienes, who surpassed himself by taking some of the best pictures of her in a white one-piece bathing costume, waving a red-spotted umbrella.

Back in Hollywood, Marilyn found more work. During 1950 five more films with her name on the cast list were released in America. There was not a lot to be said about *A Ticket to Tomahawk* (Twentieth Century-Fox), *The Fireball* (Twentieth Century-Fox) and *Right Cross* (Metro-Goldwyn Mayer), but the other two were both Hollywood film-making at its best.

Marilyn's part in John Huston's *The Asphalt Jungle,* released by Metro-Goldwyn-Mayer, was small but effective. She played Angela, the sexy 'niece' of a crooked lawyer, played by veteran actor Louis Calhern, and worked hard over the script with Natasha Lytess before doing an audition reading for John Huston. Despite her nervousness at having to do a reading for such a great director, Marilyn insisted on playing her part lying on the floor (Huston's office had no casting couch, and Angela's part involved much lying about on sofas), then insisted on doing it again when she felt her first reading had not been right.

Later, she recalled that she had seen her role in *The Asphalt Jungle* as 'a mixture of Mae West, Theda Bara and Bo-Peep – in tight silk lounging pyjamas'. The words she used were remarkably similar to Groucho Marx's description of her part in his *Love Happy,* suggesting that her later comments in a British newspaper were manufactured for her.

The Asphalt Jungle was an instant critical success when it was released, not least for its realistic and even sympathetic treatment of the gang of criminals whose activities were the film's theme. Audience reaction to Marilyn was so positive at the usual sneak

RIGHT: *A TICKET TO TOMAHAWK* was one of five films with Marilyn's name in the cast list released in 1950.

'Mr Huston was an exciting looking man. He was tall, long-faced and his hair was mussed. He was a genius — the first I had ever met.'

previews held in Hollywood, that her name, originally omitted from the credits, was re-instated before the film went on general release.

In Joseph L. Mankiewicz's *All About Eve* (Twentieth Century-Fox), Marilyn's second good film of 1950, she was really amongst the stars at last. Once again, Marilyn's role was small, but it was a good one and it was essential to the story line. She had a much more up-market image, the blonde curls were replaced with a smoothly sophisticated hairstyle and her gown was elegant and expensive.

There were two drawbacks to the great success of *All About Eve,* which won six Oscars: the whole cast was so good that Marilyn was not picked out for individual notice by critics, and, once again, she was playing a dumb blonde. She was in danger of getting type-cast. It was a danger that the Hollywood agent, Johnny Hyde, who had got Marilyn both her good parts in 1950, had foreseen.

Hyde had first noticed Marilyn in *Love Happy.* He had seen the potential in the actress and very soon had fallen in love with the girl. They made an odd couple. He was shorter than she, some thirty years older, suffered from a diseased heart – and was

'In a movie you act in little bits and pieces. You say two lines and they say 'cut'. They set up the camera in another place and you say two more lines. You walk five feet and they 'cut'. The minute you get going good in your characterization they cut. But it doesn't matter. There's no audience watching you. There's nobody to act FOR except yourself.'

'If I play a stupid girl and ask a stupid question I've got to follow it through. What am I supposed to do — look intelligent?'

'I discovered the Renaissance, met Michelangelo, Raphael and Titian [at the University of Southern California] … Finally, I decided to postpone my intelligence, but I made a promise to myself I won't forget. I promised that in a few years time when everything had settled down I would start learning – everything. I would read all the books and find out about all the wonders there were in the world.'

LEFT: *Marilyn Monroe with Jimmy Hyde, her first agent, who asked her to marry him.*

married. Hyde's wife started divorce proceedings, citing Marilyn. The divorce finalized, Hyde asked Marilyn to marry him. She refused, despite her still precarious hold on any sort of a movie career. Marriage to Hyde, a rich man, would have given her financial security and a way in to the inner circles of power in Hollywood. Her given reason was that although she cared for him very much, she did not love him. Maybe she retained a streak of naïve romanticism, or maybe she was ambitious enough to want to become someone in her own right.

When Hyde died at the end of 1950, Marilyn was deeply distressed and it would be many months before she got over his loss. But he had left her an important legacy; before his death he had negotiated a new contract for her with Twentieth Century-Fox. It was for the usual seven years, at a starting salary of $750 a week. Her immediate future was secure.

It was shortly after Hyde's death that Marilyn decided to do something serious about improving her mind. She had always been serious about reading – one-time flat-mate Shelley Winters once recalled that Marilyn was seldom seen without some weighty tome in her hand during their first year as Fox starlets. Early in the 1950s

Marilyn, with a lot of help from screenwriter and playwright Ben Hecht, wrote her 'autobiography'. Extracts were published in the popular British Sunday newspaper *Empire News* in 1954. 'Hollywood's most talked-about star, the girl 50,000 men want to marry, is writing her own story. FOR THE FIRST TIME. A story that even shock-proof Hollywood is awaiting nervously,' shouted the *Empire News*. In fact, there was not much for Hollywood to be nervous about, for Marilyn's biography turned out to follow the line put out by her studio's publicity department. It was in *Empire News,* however, that Marilyn confessed to a woeful ignorance. 'I realized that two-thirds of the time I had no idea what people were talking about,' she wrote. She said that she had enrolled in an art and literature appreciation course at the University of Southern California.

As things turned out, Marilyn did not have time to continue her education and never went back to college, but she remained serious about books and improving her mind, becoming a familiar figure in the Pickwick bookshop on Hollywood Boulevard. The main reason for the lack of time was her new contract, negotiated by Johnny Hyde, under which she began

FACING PAGE: *With George Sanders and Bette Davis in ALL ABOUT EVE (1950).*

getting much more work at Twentieth Century-Fox.

Despite the great success of *All About Eve,* Marilyn's next parts were small. However, the films were still work and gave Marilyn a base for her continuing pin-up work. She was making sure that she appeared prominently in as many magazines and newspapers as she could. The Korean War had created a big demand for pin-ups and Twentieth Century-Fox were not going to be allowed to forget that in Marilyn Monroe they had one of the most noticeably shapely pin-ups in America. Her increasing fan mail at the studio, always a great measure of a star's popularity, was soon being noticed. Part way through 1951 Fox's president, Spyros Skouras, sent out an instruction: Miss Marilyn Monroe was to be put into any current movie at the studio that had a part suited to her talents and looks. The result was appearances in three movies at Fox in 1951, and another four in 1952, as well as one for another studio. Her parts, though still far from memorable, got better with every one – apart from *Don't Bother to Knock,* in which Monroe, playing a girl made mentally unbalanced by the shock of her fiancé's death, was very wooden, indeed – and allowed her to work with such leading

'Some people have been unkind. If I say I want to grow as an actress, they look at my figure. If I say I want to develop, to learn my craft, they laugh. Somehow they don't expect me to be serious about my work.'

'I don't understand why people aren't a little more generous with each other.'

names as Cary Grant, Ginger Rogers and Charles Laughton. With the last-named she played in a sequence in *O. Henry's Full House* in which she was quite delightful playing a streetwalker to Laughton's beery old tramp.

There was one bad moment in this progress to stardom. Her loan-out film in 1952 was *Clash by Night,* made at RKO. This was a strong drama, in which the studio had invested heavily. While she was making it, a man who had noticed a girlie calendar in which the naked Monroe appeared,

---

'My sin has been no more than I have written — posing for the nude picture because I need fifty dollars desperately to get my car out of hock.'

---

stretched out on scarlet satin, had called Jerry Wald, RKO's production head, demanding money to keep quiet. It was a picture from that 1949 session with Tom Kelley, of course.

RKO and Twentieth Century-Fox were appalled. The stringent Hays Code meant most stars had morality clauses in their contracts. First reactions were to deny the whole thing, but wiser counsels prevailed. Marilyn appeared at a press conference and admitted she was the girl on the 'Golden Dreams' calendar. She played up the 'young girl alone and penniless in the big city' theme and said she had done the work to pay the rent. Someone asked if she had had anything on at all during the photography session. 'Only the radio,' replied Marilyn innocently. This first example of the wit of Marilyn Monroe went over very well and her stock soared, to go even higher when *Clash by Night* was released to good notices. Later in the year she was to win the *Look* Achievement Award for 1952, receiving it from the hands of Lauren Bacall.

By the end of 1952 Twentieth Century-Fox had decided that they must capitalize on Monroe's greatest asset, her sex appeal, and starred her in a steamy drama of marital infidelity, *Niagara.* When this was released in 1953 it made Marilyn Monroe one of the biggest box office draws in America. Even the criticism about the tight, low-cut magenta red dress Monroe wore in the film and the words of her song, 'Kiss', made for great publicity. Twentieth Century-Fox's greatest blonde asset was now Marilyn Monroe.

LEFT: *The women of middle America, in particular, were critical of Marilyn for her steamy image in NIAGARA (1953).*

PUBLIC WOMAN, PRIVATE LIFE

'There was my name up in lights. I said 'God, somebody's made a mistake. But there it was, in lights. And I sat there and said, 'Remember, you're not a star.' Yet there it was up in lights.'

FACING PAGE: *Joe DiMaggio won Marilyn Monroe's heart with his quiet, gentlemanly ways.*

IF *NIAGARA* AND ITS STAR had not pleased large numbers of American women, it had done Marilyn no harm at all. American servicemen were particularly taken with her. A group posted in the Aleutians had recently voted her 'the girl most likely to thaw Alaska'; a MASH team in Korea had chosen her 'the girl we would most like to examine'; and another group of servicemen in training had decided she was 'the girl we'd most like to climb a hill with'.

Marilyn made a personal appearance at the Pendleton Marine training camp in America, singing a few songs, dancing a little and breathing a few words into a microphone for the benefit of some 10,000

'If I'm a star, the people made me a star.'

'Gee, I never thought I had an effect on people until I was in Korea.'

whistling and cheering men, all shouting for more. She laughed at them and remarked that she could not understand why 'you boys' got so excited over sweater girls. 'Take away their sweaters and what have they got?' she asked as innocently as she had made her remark about the radio and the 'Golden Dreams' calendar.

All of which made it all the more surprising that the highly desirable Marilyn Monroe apparently had no man in her life. There had been men interested in her, but none of them, with the exception of Fred Karger, seem to have seriously interested her – apart from the playwright Arthur Miller. She had met Miller on the set of one her early films, *As Young as You Feel,* shortly after the death of Johnny Hyde and she carried on a relationship with him by letter and telephone for many months. Then, later in 1952, she met Joe DiMaggio, the great American baseball player, on a blind date. She was making *Monkey Business,* a comedy directed by Howard Hawks on which she got top billing with Cary Grant, Ginger Rogers and Charles Coburn, and invited Joe DiMaggio on to the set. Fox's publicity department arranged an off-set photo-call, at which Monroe lined up with Cary Grant and Joe DiMaggio. The press was not going to let a middle-aged movie actor come between them and a good story, and cut Cary Grant out of all the pictures. Overnight, Monroe and DiMaggio were an item.

Although she seems to have become interested in Joe quite quickly, it was a long time before either of them said anything beyond 'We are just good friends' to anyone who asked about their relationship. This was also the point at which Marilyn's career began really to take off, giving her a great deal more to think about than marriage to a retired baseball player turned businessman whose idea of an evening's entertainment was having the boys round to play cards and drink a few beers.

Niagara had been the turning point. Marilyn Monroe had been given the full star treatment, including her own on-set hairdresser and her own make-up man, Whitey Snyder, during the making of the film. She had her name – and more – above the title, too: on the billboard posters the film's name was arranged under the curves of her stretched-out body. Despite mixed reviews, the film was a big hit at the box office and Twentieth Century-Fox made a great deal of money out of it. They would no longer be able to fob off Marilyn with parts in cheap, black-and-white programmers. To do the

> '*He [Joe DiMaggio] was shy and reserved but, at the same time, rather warm and friendly. I noticed that he wasn't eating the food in front of him, that he was looking at me.*'

studio justice, they did not try to. Instead, they cannily waited six months before releasing another Monroe movie to an impatient world. This was *Gentlemen Prefer Blondes* (1953), based on Anita Loos' enormously popular book and Broadway play. The studio brought in Jane Russell to play the brunette, Dorothy.

The two women were a memorable combination on screen, acting well together and singing and dancing their way through some great musical numbers, mounted with the all-stops-out, Technicolor lavishness for which Twentieth Century-Fox was famous. Together Monroe and Russell sang two Jule Styne and Leo Robin numbers, 'Two Little Girls from Little Rock' and 'Bye Bye Baby', and 'When Love Goes Wrong' by Hoagy Carmichael and Harold Adamson. Monroe's big solo number was 'Diamonds Are a Girl's Best Friend'. It was a brilliant success – and, indeed, became a classic Monroe clip for

later television documentaries about her — partly because she got on well with the film's musical director and choreographer. Boding ill for the future, if only Fox had known, was the fact that Monroe did not get on well with director Howard Hawks.

Although *Gentlemen Prefer Blondes* was popular with movie-goers, it was coolly received by the critics, and Twentieth Century-Fox were a little hesitant about using Monroe on the revolutionary wide screen, Cinema Scope, which they invented, and the rest of Hollywood emulated to counter the growing menace of television. Fox had first used CinemaScope for a biblical epic, *The Robe,* a subject obviously well suited to wide-screen treatment. The studio was less sure about subjects needing more intimate treatment; a great deal of money would be lost if they got it wrong. Finally, Twentieth Century-Fox chose for their second venture into CinemaScope a sophisticated modern comedy, *How to Marry a Millionaire*. The stars were the studio's two greatest 'Fox blondes', Monroe and Grable, plus that sophisticated lady, Lauren Bacall.

Monroe got top billing; she also got Grable's dressing room, the biggest and most lavishly equipped on the lot. If Grable minded, she did not show it. 'Go get yours,

LEFT: *Fox had bought the film rights for Betty Grable to play in* GENTLEMEN PREFER BLONDES *(1953), but decided to cast Marilyn Monroe instead.*

it's your turn now,' she is reported to have told Marilyn. Within three months of its release at the end of 1953 *How to Marry a Millionaire* had made Twentieth Century-Fox several million dollars at the American box office, with much of the critical praise for the film being lavished on Marilyn Monroe's deliciously comic performance as the short-sighted Pola Debevoise.

In 1953 Marilyn Monroe won another award, this time for being 'the year's most popular actress'. She must have been popular, indeed, in the Twentieth Century-Fox financial department: by the end of that year she had made more money for her studio than any other female star in Hollywood.

Since several months would go by between Marilyn's completion of her work on *Millionaire* and the release of the film, Twentieth Century-Fox decided to keep her in the public eye by quickly putting her into another film. Given Marilyn's delightful performance as Pola Debevoise, it seems perverse of the studio to have decided to put her into *River of No Return* (1954), a sort of northern Western, set in the wilds of the Canadian Rockies and directed by Otto Preminger. At one point, she slipped off a raft and pulled a ligament in her foot. She was photographed on crutches, Otto

'The only thing was I couldn't get a dressing room. I said finally ... "Look, after all, I AM the blonde and it is GENTLEMEN PREFER BLONDES"'.

'An actor is supposed to be a sensitive instrument. Isaac Stern takes good care of his violin. What if everybody jumped on his violin?'

'That's the trouble, a sex symbol becomes a thing. But if I'm going to be a symbol of something, I'd rather have it sex than some other things we've got symbols of.'

'Sex is part of nature. I go along with nature.'

RIGHT: *Throughout much of the filming of* RIVER OF NO RETURN *(1954), Marilyn was required to struggle down-river on a raft with co-star Robert Mitchum.*

Preminger hovering anxiously at her side. Shaken by the incident and hating all the hearty outdoor action, Marilyn tearfully called Joe DiMaggio in California. Pausing only to collect a doctor, Joe flew to Canada to look after her, an action that touched Marilyn deeply. By the time *River of No Return* was completed Marilyn and Joe had decided on early 1954 as a date for marrying and began making plans.

Back in Hollywood from Canada, Marilyn was told that her next film was to be *The Girl in Pink Tights* (with Frank Sinatra, who was to be paid a great deal more than she because of her seven-year contract) and that she did not need to see the script in advance, just turn up for work. Monroe refused and the studio suspended her.

Marilyn Monroe and Joe DiMaggio were married in San Francisco on 14 January 1954, with enough of the world's press and TV in attendance to ensure that pictures of the newly-weds' first kiss were soon winging their way all round the world. They looked blissfully happy, but things began to go wrong very quickly. It was not just that Marilyn was not cut out for domestic life or was ever likely to be content with the quiet, stay-at-home-and-watch-television future that Joe preferred, or that she was

completely uninterested in baseball, the mainspring of Joe's life. There was also Joe's apparent indifference to the success she had achieved in Hollywood. At the end of 1953 Marilyn Monroe had been voted into fifth place, one place ahead of John Wayne, in a nation-wide poll to discover America's favourite stars; despite her current difficulties with her studio, she was still one of their biggest earning stars. In fact, she had arrived at last.

The demoralizing fact that Marilyn, not DiMaggio, America's greatest baseball player, was the one the world was interested in, was brought home to Joe when they flew to Japan, where Joe had business contacts, on an extended honeymoon in February. They were mobbed at Hawaii and again at Tokyo airport. Then she flew off to Korea, to visit American servicemen on the armistice line, leaving Joe in Japan. Her visit was a huge success, but Joe hated seeing all the pictures of her flaunting her charms in front of hundreds of servicemen.

LEFT: *Marilyn Monroe on stage, entertaining the troops in Korea.*

He also disliked her part in *There's No Business Like Show Business* (1954), the film she did for Fox when the studio lifted her suspension. Eager to get her back in work, Twentieth Century-Fox had offered her a plum part in the film version of George Axelrod's successful stage play *The Seven Year Itch* – provided she did *Show Business* first. So Marilyn Monroe, movie star, was back in work with a vengeance, leaving Joe home alone and wifeless.

There's No Business Like Show Business was, in fact, an entertaining film, bold, brassy and over-coloured with some great song and dance numbers, put over with verve and style by Ethel Merman and Donald O'Connor, in particular. Marilyn was rather out of her league and her own three big

'The only people I care about are the people in Times Square, across the street from the theatre, who can't get close as I come in. If I had light make-up on, they'd never see me. This make-up is for them ...'

numbers, especially one based on the song 'Heat Wave', were all directed in a cheaply sexy style that did nothing for her image. Middle America found her performance overly suggestive, if not downright immoral. Joe DiMaggio found himself agreeing with Middle America.

The *coup de grâce* was given the DiMaggio marriage during the making of *The Seven Year Itch,* in which Marilyn gave her finest acting performance to date. Much of the film was made in New York, and Joe went with Marilyn. He was present during the filming of its most famous scene, in which Marilyn stood on a pavement grating to let the cool air from the subway blow her pleated white skirt way up around her thighs. A great crowd gathered, Joe watched them all leering at his wife, taking photographs of her, then he walked off the set and went back to their hotel.

Marilyn was still finishing *The Seven Year Itch* in Hollywood when the break-up of her marriage to Joe DiMaggio was announced. The marriage had lasted less than ten months.

The Seven Year Itch marked a turning point in more ways than one for Marilyn. It proved to her that she did not have to be just a movie sex symbol – 'A sex symbol becomes a thing; I hate being a thing' was one of her more famous remarks of this time in her life – and it gave her the incentive to change direction. On the set of *There's No Business Like Show Business* she had made two new contacts that were to prove of enormous importance to her. One was the photographer Milton Greene, with whom she was to set up her own film production company, Marilyn Monroe Productions Inc.; the other was Paula Strasberg, wife of Lee Strasberg, co-founder of the Actors' Studio in New York.

Marilyn garnered a crop of great reviews for her work on *The Seven Year Itch,* most of them commenting on the great comic performances given by both the vastly experienced Tom Ewell and Marilyn herself.

Wrote Milton Shulman in London's *Sunday Express*: 'The test of a great film actress is whether or not she can bring something unique and individual to the imposing matter of sex. Mary Pickford brought it innocence, Theda Bara made it exotic. Marlene Dietrich made it unapproachable. Ginger Rogers gave it gaiety. Joan Crawford made it miserable, Greta Garbo lifted it to the spiritual. Ava Gardner brought it down to earth. By this standard, Miss Marilyn Monroe has certainly wiggled herself a niche in Hollywood's hall of fame. For she has made sex very funny ...'

By the time *The Seven Year Itch* was released in mid-1955 Marilyn had been living in New York for several months. Despite their divorce, Marilyn was escorted to the New York premiere by Joe DiMaggio. At this moment in her career, her position in Hollywood apparently secure, she had apparently chosen to turn her back on it. The girl who had made everyone laugh and sneer by saying that she would like to play Grushenka in *The Brothers Karamazov* demonstrated the seriousness of her desire to become a good actress by joining classes at Lee Strasberg's Actors' Studio in New York. She was not the first film actor to do so; Montgomery Clift, Rod

LEFT: *This classic image from* THE SEVEN YEAR ITCH *(1955) was also the breaking point in her relationship with Joe DiMaggio.*

'In New York I learned to make friends. Before, I never had any friends, only conquests. I didn't have the time to find real friends. I was always being looked at, had no chance to look.'

'Arthur is a serious man, but he has a wonderful sense of humour. We laugh and joke a lot.'

Steiger, Shelley Winters and Paul Newman all learned the principles of Method Acting at Lee Strasberg's feet, but she was certainly the first 'sexy Hollywood blonde' star to do so. The announcement that she had formed her own production company, Marilyn Monroe Productions Inc., with Milton Greene, came at about the same time.

She was also widening her circle of friends outside the close-knit world of movie-making. True to that earlier promise to herself that she would seek to improve her cultural background, most of her new friends came from the more intellectual stream of the world of art and literature. The Strasbergs' New York apartment became an important social base for her. Some commentators have said that it was about this time that she first met the young and handsome senator John F. Kennedy; it was certainly now that she renewed her friendship with Arthur Miller, though her growing intimacy with Miller had to be handled very discreetly, as he was still married to his first wife.

Miller kept well in the background when Marilyn returned to the West Coast to make the first film produced by her new company, Bus Stop (1956). Much more in the foreground was Paula Strasberg, who now

LEFT: *Arthur Miller announced his engagement to Marilyn Monroe while being questioned about his alleged connections with the Communist Party.*

replaced Natasha Lytess as Marilyn's drama coach. This was another film based on a play, this time by William Inge, in which Marilyn played a second-rate 'chantoosie' called Cherie.

It was a role compounded of tragedy and comedy, and Marilyn played it marvellously well, using many of the Method-based tech-

niques she had learned at the Actors' Studio. Her co-star was a virtually unknown stage actor called Don Murray, playing a gauche and innocent cowboy called Bo. His fine acting and Joshua Logan's sympathetic direction made big contributions to the warm and delightfully human story that *Bus Stop* became.

RIGHT: *In THE PRINCE AND THE SHOWGIRL (1957), Marilyn Monroe starred alongside Laurence Olivier.*

WARNER BROS. presents
LAURENCE OLIVIER · MARILYN MONROE
"THE PRINCE AND THE SHOWGIRL" (A)
with SYBIL THORNDIKE · RICHARD WATTIS · JEREMY SPENSER
TECHNICOLOR

RIGHT: *Marilyn Monroe with columnist Sheila Graham.*

The film was made under the auspices of Twentieth Century-Fox, with whom Marilyn had negotiated a new contract. She had agreed to make four films for the studio over a seven-year period; she was to be paid $100,000 a film, plus expenses, and would have script and director approval. She was also permitted under the terms of the contract to make at least one film a year outside the studio and to take on television commitments. It was a hard-headed businesswoman who had returned to Hollywood, to a huge welcome from thousands of fans.

Bus Stop opened to rave reviews for Marilyn. Typical of them was Arthur Knight's in the *Saturday Review:* 'She has submerged herself so completely in the role that one searches in vain for glimpses of the former calendar girl. It is far more than simply mastering and maintaining a ludicrous accent and intonation throughout the picture ... There is pathos, humor and a desperate pride about the girl, and Miss Monroe brings all this to life ... The real revelation in *Bus Stop* is Marilyn Monroe, and the incandescence that glows from the screen the moment she enters the story.'

By the time *Bus Stop* opened, Marilyn was in Britain to make the second film to be arranged by her own production company.

'He [Arthur Miller] wouldn't have married me if I had been nothing but a dumb blonde.'

This was *The Prince and The Showgirl* (1957) and at Marilyn's side throughout was her new husband, Arthur Miller. *The Prince and The Showgirl* was based on a play called *The Sleeping Prince* by Terence Rattigan, in which Laurence Olivier and his wife, Vivien Leigh, had had a great success on the London stage in 1953. Milton Greene had bought the film rights in the play because he was sure that Leigh's role, an actress who catches the eye of a Ruritanian prince in London for the coronation of George V in 1911, was ideal for Marilyn.

The fact that Olivier was going to reprise his stage role, as well as direct the film, caused most eyebrows to rise sharply when the project was announced at a press conference in New York. Marrying Arthur Miller was one thing – the Brain and the Body, the Egghead and the Hourglass, were typical of newspaper quips at the time – but surely Marilyn Monroe was being overly ambitious to think that she could compete on equal terms with one of the world's greatest classical actors. As filming progressed it looked as if the doubters might be right. Monroe and Olivier did not get on, while Paula Strasberg caused so many disturbances on set that Olivier banned her. Marilyn began to be hours late, to call in sick, to fail to turn up at all … For Olivier, the whole project turned into a nightmare.

In the end, a lightweight and delightfully amusing film was the result, with Marilyn giving every bit as good a performance as Olivier. The fact that she looked glowingly lovely was a tribute to the photographic skills of Milton Greene, not that she thanked him for it. Blaming him for getting her involved in the film in the first place, she bought out his share of Marilyn Monroe Productions Inc. as soon as she was back in the United States.

Although the Millers attended the New York premiere of *The Prince and the Showgirl,* they did not go to London for the British premiere. Her excuse that she had burnt her bottom sunbathing in their Long Island garden sounded unlikely. The real reason was probably that she was pregnant and did not want to endanger the baby. So the Millers settled down to married life on the East Coast of the United States.

'Movies are my business but Arthur is my life.'

MOVIE GODDESS

---

*'I don't want to play sex roles any more. I'm tired
of being known as the girl with the shape.'*

FACING PAGE: *Here, Jack Lemmon shares a late-night drink with Monroe in a sleeping car
berth during the filming of* SOME LIKE IT HOT *(1959).*

UNLIKE THE Monroe/DiMaggio relationship, the Monroe/Miller marriage went smoothly and lovingly for its first couple of years. It had its sadnesses from the beginning, however. Marilyn lost the baby she and Arthur were expecting early in 1957; it had been an ectopic pregnancy. There was another miscarriage a year or so later, followed by a minor gynaecological operation, which did not help her problem but which, like the failed pregnancies, left her depressed and unhappy.

Thinking that work might help, Arthur Miller told Marilyn that he was adapting one of his stories, called 'The Misfits', into a screenplay especially for her. He also persuaded her in 1958 to make another film with Billy Wilder, who had directed her in *The Seven Year Itch*. This time the film was a wild comedy set in the Prohibition Era, *Some Like It Hot* (1959). Her co-stars were Jack Lemmon and Tony Curtis, both of whom spent much of the film dressed as women. Because their heavy make-up looked garish in colour, the film was made in black and white, which did much to emphasize its Jazz Age setting.

Billy Wilder, who with I.A.L. Diamond wrote the film's witty and sophisticated script, was to remark later that he deserved

LEFT: *Despite her marriage to Arthur Miller, for Marilyn Monroe the late 1950s were difficult years.*

some sort of medal – the Purple Heart would do – for directing Monroe twice, while Tony Curtis famously said that making love to her in *Some Like It Hot* was 'like kissing Hitler'. Told of his remark later, Marilyn riposted, 'He only said that about "kissing Hitler" because I wore prettier dresses than he did.' Much later, in the course of her last taped interview, for *Life's* Richard Meryman, a more paranoid Marilyn brought up Curtis's remark – downgrading him to 'some actor' – to make the point that when making movies she was working hard, not indulging some pleasant relationship with a fellow actor. If her fellow actors could not accept this, then that was their problem.

In truth, making *Some Like It Hot* had been another nightmare for all concerned. Marilyn was often late, often sick, often not on set at all; when she was, she seemed unable to remember the simplest line and there had to be take after take of many scenes. Towards the end of filming, Marilyn was pregnant again, which no doubt affected her work. The miracle was that out of this seemingly awful experience came one of the funniest, most poignant and most joyously spontaneous films ever to be made in Hollywood.

Once again, Marilyn was cast as a singer, Sugar Kane, working in an all-girl band, Sweet Sue's Society Syncopaters. In the course of the film she sang three songs in her inimitable, little-girl whispery way: 'Running Wild' by Joe Gray and Leo Worth, 'I Wanna Be Loved By You' by Bert Kalmar, Harry Ruby and Herbert Stothart, and 'I'm Through With Love' by Gus Kahn, Matty Malneck and F. Livingston.

'I am invariably late for appointments – sometimes as much as two hours. I've tried to change my ways but the things that make me late are too strong, and too pleasing.'

The film was an instant success, earning a great deal of money for its producers, Mirisch Productions and United Artists. As for Marilyn's performance, *Variety* said 'She is a comedienne with that combination of sex appeal and timing that just can't be beat.' For Archer Winsten in the *New York Post,* 'Marilyn does herself proud.'

'I don't mind making jokes but I don't want to look like one.'

Marilyn was not to work on another film until 1960. This time she was back under Twentieth Century-Fox's wing, to do a modern romantic comedy, with a screen-play by Norman Krasna and additional material by Hal Kanter (and some tinkering on Marilyn's behalf by Arthur Miller), in which she starred with French actor and singer Yves Montand. The film, *Let's Make Love* (1960), given the script writers and the fact that it was to be directed by the immensely experienced George Cukor – a 'woman's director' if ever there was one – should have been good. It turned out to be a fairly slight affair.

Marilyn, playing a singer called Amanda Dell working in an off-Broadway theatrical group, had little to do but look lovely and sing several songs, including Cole Porter's 'My Heart Belongs to Daddy', which she did as if in rehearsal, wearing black leotards and a heavy Aran-knit sweater. For the film reviewer of London's *Time Out* magazine,

LEFT: *LET'S MAKE LOVE (1960) was the sort of simple backstage story that is so popular in Hollywood musicals.*

Marilyn's entrance down a fireman's pole for the song gave *Let's Make Love* its one moment of true magic; otherwise, it was 'not so much a good film as a delightful experience'.

When she started work on this film, Marilyn's marriage to Arthur Miller was going through a bad patch. By the time the film was finished, it looked as if the marriage was, too. Marilyn made no secret of her attraction to Yves Montand, going so far as to say at a press conference that she thought him, next to her husband and alongside Marlon Brando, the most attractive man she had ever met. Despite her protestations that there was nothing between her and Montand, who 'is a married man', there seems no doubt that during the making of the film she had an affair with him, to the great distress of his wife, actress Simone Signoret.

Once the film was made, Montand went back to France with his wife, who chose to forgive and forget rather than destroy her marriage, and Monroe and Miller, outwardly at least, carried on with their marriage too. From Twentieth Century-Fox's point of view, the publicity the affair had garnered was no bad thing: *Let's Make Love* needed all the help it could get. General reaction to

'[Hollywood is] a place where they'll pay you a thousand dollars for a kiss and fifty cents for your soul.'

'Men who think that a woman's past love affairs lessen her love for them are usually stupid and weak. A woman can bring a new love to each man she loves, providing there are not too many.'

ABOVE: *It seems certain
that Marilyn Monroe had
an affair with Yves
Montand during filming of
LET'S MAKE LOVE (1960).*

Marilyn's performance was probably best summed up by *Time* magazine's review: 'There is a lot of Marilyn to admire these days, but it is still in fine fettle; at thirty-four she makes twenty-one look ridiculous. The smile that reassures nervous males ("It's all right, I'm not real") has never been more dazzling. And the comic counter-point of fleshy grandeur and early Shirley Temple manner is better than ever.'

Let's Make Love out of the way, Marilyn and Arthur Miller started work almost as once on *The Misfits*. Miller had sent his completed screenplay to John Huston two years before, and the director was very impressed with it, as were the actors – Clark Gable, Montgomery Clift and Eli Wallach – to whom the script was also sent. They were all quickly signed up for the film, although it would be nearly two years before they were all free of commitments at the same time and could start work. Thus it was not until July 1960 that cast and crew for *The Misfits* assembled in Nevada. The script they were about to make into a film which John Huston, at least, thought would be a major work and a box-office success, was based on a short story by Arthur Miller about three cowboys who captured wild horses for sale to dog-food manufacturers. He built up a

female part that had been minor in the short story into a major role for Marilyn. John Huston, summing up the story later, described it as a story about people 'who aren't willing to sell their lives. They will sell their work but they won't sell their lives and for that reason they are misfits.'

'He [Arthur Miller] is a wonderful writer, a brilliant man. But I think he is a better writer than a husband.'

Marilyn played Roslyn Taber, a New York woman in Reno to get a divorce. In a state of emotional turmoil herself, she is introduced first to Guido (Eli Wallach), a cowboy saddened by the death of his wife, then to an ageing but still attractive cowboy, Gay Langland (Clark Gable), emotionally scarred by the failure of his relationship with his own children. Also involved in the horse round-up Gable is organizing is a rodeo rider, Perce Howland (Montgomery Clift), who proves to be past his best when he is

'Everybody is always tugging at you. They'd all like a sort of chunk out of you. I don't think they realize it, but it's like "grrrr do this, grrrr do that ..." But you do want to stay intact — intact and on two feet.'

hurt while taking part in a local rodeo. A major scene in the film, involving the actors in great physical and emotional stress, centres on Roslyn's attempt to set free the horses already captured when she discovers that these beautiful creatures are to be killed for dog food.

Despite Monroe's presence, the film in John Huston's hands became very much a study of male character, of men needing the love of a woman but strong enough to function on their own, even to face death, without fear. As Gay Langland said, in words written for him by Arthur Miller, 'We've all got to go sometime, dying's as natural as living. A man who's afraid to die is afraid to live.' Sadly prophetic words, these, for Clark Gable died of a heart attack in November 1960, just weeks after finishing his part in *The Misfits*.

It would be Marilyn Monroe's last completed film too. Throughout its making she had been in a bad way, physically and psychologically — a fact she apparently recognized herself when she remarked of her fellow actor Montgomery Clift, 'He is the only person I know who's in worse shape than I am.' When she spoke to Miller at all — which, from all accounts, was not often as she would not even ride to the set in the same car as her husband — it was usually to argue with him about the script. It did not take her long to see that the part he had written specially for her was turning out to be still a minor one, with less reality than Gable's role. 'He could have written me anything,' she said sadly. 'If that's what he thinks of me, well, then I'm not for him and he's not for me.'

In justice to Miller it should be said that Monroe was almost certainly out of sympathy with John Huston too, fully aware he was far from being a woman's director; she probably felt very alone in this man's world, with only Paula Strasberg to back her up artistically. The one bright spot in all this was the presence of Clark Gable, an actor whom she had idolized since girlhood

FACING PAGE: Marilyn starred with Montgomery Clift and Clark Gable in THE MISFITS *(1961).*

'It stirs up envy, fame does. People ... feel fame gives them some kind of privilege to walk up to you and say anything to you – and it won't hurt your feelings – like it's happening to your clothing.'

and who now fully lived up to the image she had of him: 'a gentleman – the best,' she said of him.

Marilyn Monroe's chronic lack of confidence in herself and her sheer terror of film-making led her to seek relief in drugs. Her dependence on them was such that there were times on set when she could hardly speak coherently, whole days on which she did not appear at all. There was even an occasion when the cameraman told Huston they would have to stop because Marilyn's eyes were not focused. Part way through filming she had to return to Los Angeles for treatment in a private clinic to get her off the huge doses of barbiturates she had been taking. In the end it was not until late in October that filming in the heat of the Nevada desert was completed and the exhausted cast and crew could return to Los Angeles.

The Misfits was released in February 1961 to generally mixed reviews. Marilyn's role was seen by most critics as impossible, though, as the reviewer for *The Times* newspaper said, 'given a completely impossible part to play, [she] makes it credible, if hardly likeable, by the sheer strength of her own passionate identification with the character. Considerations of whether she can really act seem as irrelevant as they were with Garbo; it is her rare gift just to *be* in front of the camera.'

Few saw *The Misfits* as the great film John Huston had anticipated. It 'is a dozen pictures rolled into one. Most of them, unfortunately, are terrible ...' said *Time* magazine. 'It is an honest but clumsy western, a pseudosociological study of the American cowboy in the last, disgusting stages of obsolescence, a raucous ode to Reno and the horrors of divorce ... and, above all, a glum, long ... fatuously embarrassing psychoanalysis of Marilyn Monroe, Arthur Miller and what went wrong with their famous marriage.'

Time magazine was able to write of the Monroe/Miller marriage in the past tense because Marilyn had announced in November 1960, just weeks after filming had been finished, that her marriage to Arthur Miller was over. She went to Mexico for the divorce, flying to Juarez on 20 January 1961, the day John F. Kennedy was inaugurated President of the United States, in the hopes that the world's press would be more interested in Kennedy than her. She was wrong; word had gone out and enough pressmen were on hand to ensure that news of the ending her marriage to Arthur Miller was common knowledge within hours.

The marriage was to be Marilyn Monroe's last long-term stable relationship. Arthur Miller was more lucky. Left emotionally battered and exhausted by the last hideous months of his marriage, he failed to recognize the woman who was to give him a much happier relationship when he bumped into her in New York one day. He knew she had been one of the great crowd of press people attending the filming of *The Misfits* in Nevada, but he had to call a friend to be reminded that she was Magnum photographer Inge Morath. Their friendship blossomed and quite soon they were married. Their first child was born just weeks after Marilyn's death in 1962.

LEFT: *Marilyn Monroe sings 'Happy Birthday' at a gala concert marking President Kennedy's forty-fifth birthday.*

It was here that she is believed to have met the Kennedy brothers.

Early in 1962 she at last started work on a new film for Twentieth Century-Fox, to whom she was still contracted. The film was called *Something's Got to Give* and her co-star was to be Dean Martin, another member of the Rat Pack. The director was once again George Cukor – though even he had never experienced the terrible time he was to have on the very few days he managed to get Marilyn Monroe in front of his camera.

All too soon the old Monroe problems resulted in lateness, rudeness to director and crew, sickness, and no-shows on a scale never before experienced by the studio. The last straw for Twentieth Century-Fox came when Marilyn called in sick and then flew off to New York to sing 'Happy Birthday' to President Kennedy on the occasion of a gala all-star concert at Madison Square Garden to mark his forty-fifth birthday, an event to which she was escorted by her ex-father-in-law, Isadore Miller. Back in Hollywood, Marilyn celebrated her own thirty-sixth birthday on 1 June with a party, complete with large birthday cake, on the set of *Something's Got to Give,* and a visit to the Los Angeles Dodgers Ball Park for a charity event. A couple of days later she called in

'I feel stronger if the people around me on the set love me, care for me, and hold good thoughts for me. It creates an aura of love, and I believe I can give a better performance.'

'We did some test scenes of me in a pool, sort of nude. I hope they give me some good nude lines to go with it.'

sick again and Twentieth Century-Fox's patience snapped. The studio fired her for 'wilful violation' of her contract, scrapped the film and slapped a $500,000 lawsuit on Marilyn Monroe Productions Inc.

For two months after her sacking Marilyn continued outwardly to pursue the life of a busy movie star. There were visits to the Lawford house, where it was suggested that she carried on an affair with Robert Kennedy several months after her affair with the President. No one has ever revealed the truth about these affairs. Common knowledge of President Kennedy's womanizing, however, has suggested to many that Marilyn was just a 'trophy woman' to him, whereas to Robert Kennedy she was perhaps more – though never enough for him to cut himself off from his family.

Partly in pursuit of a publicity campaign aimed at getting herself reinstated at

'I'm looking forward to eventually becoming a marvellous – excuse the word marvellous – character actress.'

Twentieth Century-Fox, Marilyn went back to 'making Marilyns'. As we have seen, the men behind the cameras were Bert Stern, Douglas Kirkland and George Barris. The results of their collaboration were some of the most candidly sexy photographs of a leading movie star ever taken. Far from the near-pornography of some present-day 'star' photography, they were just warmly, lovingly, Marilyn. There is no denying, though, that the woman in these photographs is no longer young.

Marilyn had always known that she could not remain a cinema sex goddess for ever, but the progress to great actress, even character actress, as she had once said she hoped to become, seemed to have stalled in that summer of 1962. Signs of a neurotic desperation were showing in her behaviour. She was threatening to go public over her alleged affairs with the Kennedys. She was still relying heavily on her psychiatrist, her doctor and a great many other people to keep her on the right side of the line between mental health and breakdown. In her small, still only half-furnished house in Los Angeles she would spend hours on the phone calling friends all over the United States. During the night of 4/5 August 1962 the balance apparently shifted drastically.

LEFT: *Marilyn Monroe with Rock Hudson at the Golden Globe ceremony in March 1962, five months before her death.*

Either accidentally or deliberately, she took an overdose of barbiturates and died. When the police arrived, called in by her house-keeper, Eunice Murray, and Dr Greenson, the telephone was still in her hand.

Although the Los Angeles county coroner's publicly announced verdict on the death of Marilyn Monroe was that it was 'the result of barbiturate poisoning' and 'probably suicide', many rumours were soon circulating around the body of the world's most famous female movie star. Numerous people came forward to say they had seen Robert Kennedy, believed to have been staying with friends near San Francisco on 4 August, actually in Los Angeles, where he was said to have visited Marilyn. It was soon being said that he had ended their affair that afternoon, thus causing the depression that led to her suicide.

Over the years, the rumours became wilder, blacker. She had been murdered, perhaps on the orders of Robert Kennedy to stop her going public about her affairs with him and his brother ... She had killed herself as a result of the depression caused by a fourth abortion, this one to prevent the birth of an illegitimate child of the President of the United States ... She had been killed by the CIA, the Mafia, even the FBI ...

Twenty years later, in 1982, the Los Angeles District Attorney re-opened the police investigation into the death of Marilyn Monroe. His staff spent four months sifting through the mountain of evidence, then advised him that it 'failed to support any theory of criminal conduct'. In this same year Joe DiMaggio cancelled the order he had made twenty years before for fresh roses always to be placed in front of Marilyn's tomb in Westwood cemetery. It was as if he were saying to the world that the time had come for a line to be drawn under Marilyn's death, for her to become simply a memory.

One of the last big interviews Marilyn gave was to Richard Meryman of *Life* magazine. From eight hours of tape he got a strikingly candid interview, published in *Life* on 3 and 17 August 1962 and then, thirty years later, as a television programme, with Marilyn's hauntingly alive voice and laugh played over a series of stills and film clips. During the interview she had told Meryman, 'I now live for my work and the few relationships with the few people I can really count on. Fame will go by and, so long, I've had you, Fame ... So, at least it's something I've experienced, but that's not where I live.'

RIGHT: *Signs of grief were clear on Joe DiMaggio's face at the funeral of Marilyn Monroe.*

RIGHT: *Far from fading, memories of Marilyn Monroe stay bright; even today, fans still place fresh roses at her crypt.*